40/ U7 8886
24-10-97 UBS

Mithai

A Collection of Traditional Indian Sweets

Mithai

A Collection of Traditional

Indian Sweets

Pramila Parmar

 **UBSPD**

UBS Publishers' Distributors Ltd.
New Delhi Bombay Bangalore Madras
Calcutta Patna Kanpur London

UBS Publishers' Distributors Ltd.

5 Ansari Road, New Delhi-110 002
Phones : 3273601, 3266646 ✗ *Cable* : ALLBOOKS ✗ *Fax* : (91) 11-327-6593
E-mail: ubspd.del@smy.sprintrpg.ems.vsnl.net.in

Apeejay Chambers, 5 Wallace Street, Mumbai-400 001
Phones : 2076971, 2077700 ✗ *Cable* : UBSIPUB ✗ *Fax* : 2070827

10 First Main Road, Gandhi Nagar, Bangalore-560 009
Phones : 2263901, 2263902, 2253903 ✗ *Cable* : ALLBOOKS ✗ *Fax* : 2263904

6, Sivaganga Road, Nungambakkam, Chennai-600 034
Phone : 8276355 ✗ *Cable* : UBSIPUB ✗ *Fax* : 8270189

8/1-B, Chowringhee Lane, Calcutta-700 016
Phones : 2441821, 2442910, 2449473 ✗ *Cable* : UBSIPUBS ✗ *Fax* : 2450027

5 A, Rajendra Nagar, Patna-800 016
Phones : 652856, 653973, 656170 ✗ *Cable* : UBSPUB ✗ *Fax* : 656169

80, Noronha Road, Cantonment, Kanpur-208 004
Phones : 369124, 362665, 357488 ✗ *Fax* : 315122

© Pramila Parmar

First Published	**1994**
First Reprint	**1995**
Second Reprint	**1996**
Third Reprint	**1997**

Cover Design : UBS Art Studio

Lasertypeset in 11 pt. Times and printed at
Replika Press (P) Ltd. Delhi

INTRODUCTION

MITHAI, also known as Mishthaan — meaning 'Mist Ann' or sweet food, is synonymous with happiness, gaiety and celebration. Every happy occasion of Indian life revolves around sweets—be it a birth, marriage, festival or any good news. We have special sweets for every celebration.

The exotic, fascinating and mouth watering varietiy of sweets from different parts of the country is something Indians should be proud of. This culinary heritage, which has been passed down from generation to generation needs to be preserved. There are many times when one wishes to have some knowledge of this culinary expertise to make something special and appropriate for the occasion.

In this book I have tried to cover a wide range of traditional sweets from all over India. There are easy to make, step by step recipes for beginners as well as some more intricate ones for the more experienced ones.

New Delhi   **Pramila Parmar**

CONTENTS

Glossary of Indian Words

Almonds	—	*Badam*
Bengal gram or gram flour	—	*Besan*
Brown cardamom	—	*Bari Elaychi*
Buffalo Milk	—	*Bhens Ka Doodh*
Cardamoms	—	*Elaychi*
Cashew nuts	—	*Kaju*
Coconut	—	*Nariyal*
Fresh coconut	—	*Taaza Nariyal*
Desiccated coconut	—	*Sookhe Nariyal Ka Bura*
Cottage cheese	—	*Paneer*
Cow Milk	—	*Gaai Ka Doodh*
Green Gram	—	*Chilke Wali Moong Ki Dal*
Molasses or Jaggery	—	*Gur*
Nutmeg	—	*Jaiphal*
Pista or Pistachio	—	*Pista*
Poppy seeds	—	*Khus khus*
Peanuts	—	*Moongphalli*
Raisins	—	*Kishmis*
Refined flour	—	*Maida*
Saffron	—	*Kesar or Zafran*
Semolina	—	*Rawa or Sooji*
Sesame	—	*Til*
Silver sheets	—	*Chandi Ka Vark*
Sweetened Milk	—	*Rabri*
Tartaric Powder	—	*Nimbu Ke Sat Ka Powder*
Tartary	—	*Nimbu Ka Sat*
Top cream of the milk	—	*Malai*
Wheat Flour	—	*Atta*
White gram	—	*Dhuli Urd Ki Dal*
White pumpkin	—	*Saphed Kaddu*

Commonly Used Traditional Words

Alfonso or Aapus   —   A special variety of mango

Boondi fryer or strainer   —   A round metal sieve with
                                 small holes and handle

Chakka   —   Semi dehydrated curd. Water
                                 is removed from the fresh
                                 curd by hanging it in a
                                 muslin cloth for few hours.

Charmagaz   —   Mixed peeled seeds of cucumber,
                                 watermelon, pumpkin and muskmelon.

Chironji   —   A type of dry fruit obtained
                                 from the inside of the seed
                                 of a berry type of fruit.

Dashari   —   A special variety of mango

Ghee   —   Clarified butter of hydrogenated
                                 vegetable fat.

Karahi   —   Half circled metal utensil
                                 with rings on two sides on
                                 the top. Specially used for frying.

Khoya or Mawa   —   Reduced milk

Lavang   —   Clove

Mithai   —   Sweetmeat

Reetha   —   A type of round dried nut with
                                 lathering property

Sonth   —   Dried ginger

Common Processes Used in Sweet-Making

DECORATION WITH ICING

Prepare the khoya cheese or Cream icing. Add the colour and essence as desired. Fill this in the icing bag or gun used in cake decoration. Fit in the bag with a star shaped nozzle. Decorate cottage cheese based sweets with this icing. Press the icing through the nozzle into fancy flowers and borders as done in cake icing.

DECORATION WITH SILVER SHEETS

These are very fine, thin foils of silver prepared by beating and rolling silver pieces. The sheets are so thin that they are spread and stored on sheets of paper kept one over the other.

To use them lift a sheet of paper along with the silver sheet, turn it on to the surface to be decorated. Neatly press and smoothen paper all along. Remove the paper. The silver sheet will be evenly spread on the surface. Never directly touch the silver sheet, otherwise it will stick to the fingers.

For sticking silver bits use the same method of lifting and spreading along with the paper. Fake silver sheets are made out of aluminium, and turn brown even when stored for a short duration. They are harmful. A real silver sheet will retain its colour and shine.

MAKING SUGAR SYRUP

Sugar syrups of varying thickness are used in sweet-making. There are a few basic rules to make a perfect sugar syrup required in the recipe-

1. The utensils used should be clean, without any trace of fat. Presence of fats affects setting of sugar.

2. Measure the quantity of sugar given into cups. Usually add 1/2 cup less water than the sugar unless specified in the recipe. For example if $2\frac{1}{2}$ cups (500 gms) of sugar is used in the recipe, add 2 cups (400 ml) of water to make the syrup.

3. Always boil the sugar-water mixture on medium flame. If there are traces of dirt in the sugar, it is advisable to clean it. Add 2 - 3 tablespoons of milk or a teaspoon of lemon juice in the boiling syrup. The dirt will precipitate. The syrup then should be strained through a fine strainer. Reboil the syrup to the desired consistency.

4.   Do not stir the syrup unnecessarily or too frequently once the sugar is dissolved in water.

5.   Once the sugar-water mixture starts boiling check for the required consistency :-

No string syrup— The boiling syrup is not sticky or minimum sticky. The syrup when trickled down from a tilted spoon shows no string. If falls in a thin stream.

One string syrup— Further boiling of no string syrup for 2 - 3 minutes will give one string syrup. It will fall in drops when poured slowly from a spoon. The syrup is slightly sticky when felt between two fingers. Boiling for another minute or two will give $1\frac{1}{2}$ string syrup which is used in many of the sweets.

Two string syrup— Boil the $1\frac{1}{2}$ string syrup further for a minute or two. The syrup will thicken. When dropped gradually from a tilted spoon two drops will fall at a time. Place few drops of syrup in a plate. Let them cool and then tilt the plate. The drops will move heavily and will crease. The syrup when felt between two fingers will give double threads. This consistency is used in most of the recipes. Boil the syrup slightly more for 1/2 a minute. This will give $2\frac{1}{2}$ string syrup which is also known as soft ball stage. When cooled or put in cold water the drops will form into a soft sugar ball. This syrup is also commonly used in making sweets.

Three string syrup— Boil $2\frac{1}{2}$ string syrup for another minute or so and the syrup will be really thick. When dropped from a tilted spoon, it will fall into flakes. The drops when cooled will crease heavily and in cold water will form a hard ball. This is mostly used in sweets for giving sugar coating.

USING A BOONDI STRAINER

A boondi strainer or fryer is a flat or cup-like metal sieve attached to a handle. The size of the holes vary from very small, medium to large. The selection will depend on the size of boondi required. Fill the boondi batter in the cup-like sieve. Hit the cup-like strainer with a heavy spoon, into the karahi on the fire. The boondies will fall into the hot ghee. In case you are using the flat strainer, position it over the karahi, pour batter into it and hit it at the edges of the karahi. The boondies will drop into the hot ghee.

TYPES OF KHOYA

Khoya or mawa is prepared by boiling and reducing the milk to a semi-solid stage. There are different types depending upon the use of ingredients and moisture content.

1.   **Batti ka khoya**— This is solid and moulded khoya. It is made out of full cream buffalo milk. The milk is boiled in a large karahi on a high flame, and stirred occasionally. The flame is reduced when the milk thickens. When the mixture is in a semi-solid stage it is

removed from the fire and set into moulds. A litre of milk will yield 200 grams of khoya. This khoya is used in burfies and laddus.

2. **Daab ka or chikna khoya**— This is made with low fat buffalo milk. The process of making it is the same as for batti ka khoya but it is removed from the fire slightly earlier. It is loose and sticky in consistency with a higher moisture content. It is suitable for making gulab-jamuns and gajar ka halwa.

3. **Danedar or granulated khoya**— This khoya is made out of full cream buffalo milk. The difference is that khoya is curdled slightly by adding little tartary in powder form. The milk curdles slightly hence the khoya is soft textured and coarse like cottage cheese. Care should be taken not to spoil the texture while stirring. The water content is more than batti ka khoya but less then the chikna khoya. This type is used in making kalakand and laddu.

USE OF KHOYA AND COTTAGE CHEESE CRUMBS

They are generally used to beautify cottage cheese-based sweets. Rub granulated khoya with the palms. Roast it in a karahi on medium flame. Remove from the fire when the mixture dries up. Cool the mixture and again rub with the palms to get a crumb-like texture. Cottage cheese crumbs are also prepared in the same way. To use these crumbs spread them thinly and evenly on a plate and roll the sweet over to coat it with the crumbs.

MEASUREMENT OF LIQUIDS

All the weights and measurements used in this book are in metric system that is in grams and litres. For the convenience of the readers, however, water and milk measurements are also given in cups. One cup is being equal to 200 ml of liquid.

BURFIS

An Assortment of Sweets

Pedas, Cashew tarts with Khoya filling

An Assortment of Sweets

KHOYA BURFI

Requirements

500 gms	**khoya**
250-300 gms	**powdered sugar**
2/3 teaspoons	**cardamom powder**

For decoration : 1/3 teaspoon cardamom powder, 2 teaspoons chopped pistas, 2 silver sheets.

Steps

1. Grate the khoya. Mix with the sugar. Put in a karahi and cook on a slow fire till the mixture is semi-solid. Remove from the fire.

2 When cold, mix in the cardamom powder and spread the mixture evenly on a greased metal tray. It should be about 1½" thick.

3. Sprinkle cardamom powder and chopped pista all over. Press on silver sheets. Cut into medium sized squares. When set, lift out the pieces and store.

Varieties :

By adding a few ingredients to the basic khoya burfi, the following varieties can be made.

CASHEW BURFI

Add 100 gms finely chopped cashewnuts and 50 gms powdered sugar to the khoya mixture while roasting. Prepare and decorate burfi in the same manner.

ALMOND BURFI

Mix 80 gms finely chopped almonds and 40 gms powdered sugar to the khoya mixture while roasting. Apart from the normal decoration, spread 20 gms chopped almonds.

PISTA BURFI

Add 50 gms chopped pistas to the khoya mixture after removing from fire. Decorate in the usual way.

Makes 30 pieces.

Contd. . . . .

WALNUT BURFI

Prepare this only during winter. Add 100 gms chopped walnuts to the khoya mixture after removing from the fire. Also add 50 gms extra powdered sugar to the khoya mixture, while roasting.

TUTTI FRUTTI OR CHERRY BURFI

Mix 100 gms chopped tutti frutti or cherries to the khoya mixture, after it is removed from the fire. Set the burfi in the usual way.

FLAVOURED AND COLOURED BURFIES

Make pineapple burfi by mixing 1/2 teaspoon of pineapple essence and 3/4 teaspoon of pineapple colour to the cold khoya burfi mixture. Set the burfi and decorate only with silver sheets.

In the same way, prepare orange, lemon, mango, banana, raspberry, strawberry and rose burfies by mixing colours and essences to the basic khoya mixture. Varieties can be obtained by cuttings burfies in different shapes and sizes.

For preparing double and multicoloured burfies, prepare different coloured khoya mixtures with matching flavours. Spread one layer on top of the other. Decorate with silver sheets and cut into strips.

KESARI BURFI

Dissolve 10 - 12 strands of saffron in a little milk. Add this to the burfi mixture before setting it. Along with silver sheets, decorate a few strands of saffron on the burfi. 1/2 teaspoon of orange colour can also be added if desired.

NUTMEG BURFI

Dissolve 1/2 teaspoon of nutmeg powder in a table spoon of milk. Add this to the khoya mixture before setting the burfi. Decorate with Pistas and silver sheets. Cut into pieces.

CHOCOLATE BURFI

This is usually made in a double colour. Divide the basic burfi mixture into two. To one, add cardamom powder. Into the other, mix 3 tablespoons of cocoa powder and 1/2 teaspoon chocolate colour. Arrange the layers one over the other, evenly. Keep the chocolate layer on top. Spread silver sheets on top and cut into pieces.

CARROT BURFI

Requirements

1 kg	**carrots, washed, peeled and grated**
1 litre	**milk (full cream)**
450 gms	**sugar**
150 gms	**khoya**
100 gms	**ghee**

For decoration : 2 teaspoons chopped pistas, 2 tablespoons chopped cashew nuts, 1 tablespoon chopped almond, 1/2 teaspoon cardamom powder

Steps

1. Cook grated carrots and milk in a karahi, on a medium flame. When the mixture dries up, reduce the flame and keep stirring.

2. Add the sugar and cook till the mixture dries up. Keep stirring.

3. Add the grated khoya and ghee. Fry till it becomes semi-solid.

4. Turn the mixture on to a greased metal tray. Press down evenly and decorate with dry fruits and cardamom.

5. Cut into diamond shaped pieces.

Makes 45-50 pieces

CHIRONJI BURFI

Requirements

100 gms	chironji
75 gms	ghee
100 gms	khoya
125 gms	powdered sugar

For decoration:

1 silver sheet

Steps

1. Soak chironji in water for 20 minutes. Drain and grind it coarsely.

2. Heat ghee in a karahi. Fry the chironji paste on a medium to slow flame. Keep stirring.

3. When the mixture turns brown in colour and the ghee separates add the mashed khoya.

4. Fry for 5-7 minutes. Remove from the fire.

5. Add the sugar powder when the mixture is cold. Keep for 10 minutes. Mix well and spread on a greased tray. The layer should be 1-1½" thick. Decorate with the silver sheet. Cut into pieces.

Makes 16 pieces.

DIL KHUSHAL BURFI

Requirements

500 gms	**gramflour**
100 gms	**ghee**
$\frac{1}{2} - \frac{3}{4}$ cup	**water**
500 gms	**khoya**
250 gms	**ghee**
125 gms	**fresh curds**
600 gms	**sugar**
$2\frac{1}{2}$ cups	**water**

For decoration: 2-3 silver sheets, 25 gms char magaz, 1/2 teaspoon cardamom powder

Steps

1. Rub 100 gms ghee into the gramflour.

2. Gradually add the water and prepare a very tight dough. Divide it into five equal balls. Flatten them.

3. Mash the khoya and roast it in a karahi to a light pink colour . Remove and let it cool.

4. Heat the ghee in the karahi. Fry the gram balls on a medium to slow flame. When they are brown in colour and crisp remove them. Crush them evenly to a bread-crumb like texture.

5. Add the beaten curds, and fry till the water evaporates and the mixture dries up.

6. Add the khoya to this mixture and remove from the fire.

7. In the meantime, prepare a 2½ string syrup with sugar and water.

8. Add this syrup to the gramflour mixture. Turn onto a greased metal tray. Press down evenly.

9. Decorate with silver sheets and cut into pieces when set.

Makes 60-70 pieces.

FRESH COCONUT BURFI

Requirements

1	**fresh coconut (about 700-800 gms)**
1 litre	**buffalo milk**
350 gms	**sugar**

For decoration : $\frac{1}{2}$ teaspoon cardamom powder, 1 teaspoon chopped pista.

Steps:

1. Grate the fresh coconut finely.

2. Mix together the milk, coconut and sugar, in a thick bottomed karahi.

3. Cook on a high flame. Stir occasionally. When the mixture thickens, reduce the flame to minimum. Keep stirring.

4. When the mixture becomes semi-solid, remove from the fire. Spread on a greased surface to a thickness of 1-2".

5. Decorate with pista and cardamoms. Cut into pieces.

Varieties: Use red, yellow, orange and green food colours to prepare coloured burfies.

Makes 25-30 pieces.

MANGO BURFI

Requirements

250 gms	**ripe mango pulp (Alfonso or Dashari)**
250 gms	**powdered sugar**
250 gms	**khoya**

For decoration : $\frac{1}{2}$ teaspoon cardamom powder, 2 tablespoons chironji, 1 teaspoon chopped pistas, 1 tea spoon chopped tuttifrutti, 6 - 8 drops orange colour

Steps

1. Mix together the mango pulp and 100 gms sugar. Cook in a thick vessel till reduced by half.

2. Grate the khoya and fry it in a karahi on a medium flame. When it is light pink in colour, add the remaining sugar and mango pulp. Cook for 5 - 7 minutes, till the mixture is semi-solid. Remove from the fire.

3. Mix in orange colour evenly.

4. Prepare small mango shaped burfies, with greased palms and fingers.

5. Decorate with chironji, cardamom, pista and tuttifrutti.

Makes 24 pieces.

CHANNA DAL BURFI

Requirements:

250 gms	**bengal gram**
1 fresh	**coconut, grated**
125 gms	**ghee**
1 litre	**milk**
500 gms	**sugar**

For decoration : $\frac{1}{2}$ teaspoon cardamom powder, 2 silver sheets

Steps

1. Soak the gram in water over night

2. Drain and grind it to a thick fine paste using little water.

3. Grate and roast the coconut to a pink colour. Keep aside.

4. Heat ghee in a karahi and fry the gram paste in it on a medium flame, till the moisture dries up.

5. When the mixture separates from the ghee, add the sugar, milk and coconut.

6. stir and cook till the mixture is thick and leaves the sides of the Karahi.

7. Turn on to a greased tray Spread evenly. Decorate with cardamom powder and silver sheets. Cut into pieces.

Makes 30 pieces.

CHAR MAGAZ BURFI

Requirements

100 gms	char magaz seeds
200 gms	grated dry coconut
500 gms	sugar
2 cups	water
50 gms	chironji
50 gms	chopped cashew nuts

For decoration : $\frac{1}{2}$ tea spoon cardamom powder, 2 silver sheets.

Steps:

1. Roast char magaz seeds in a karahi. In 5 -7 minutes, they will become light and fluffy.

2. Roast the dry coconut to a pink colour.

3. Boil the sugar and water. Prepare a two string syrup

4. Add the rest of the ingredients. Cook for 2-3 minutes. When the mixture leaves the sides of the karahi, remove it at once.

5. Immediately turn on to a greased metal tray. Press down evenly.

6. Decorate with cardamom and silver sheets. Cut in to squares with a greased knife.

Makes 30-35 pieces.

MOONG DAL BURFI

Requirements

250 gms	**green gram**
200 gms	**ghee**
250 gms	**sugar**
250 ml	**milk**

For decoration : 2 tablespoons mixed chopped dry fruits like pistas and almonds, $\frac{1}{2}$ teaspoon cardamom powder. 2 silver sheets

Steps

1. Soak the gram in water overnight.

2. Rub and wash it, removing the outer green skin.

3. Drain the gram and grind it to a thick paste using little water.

4. Heat ghee in a karahi. Add the paste and fry it on a medium to slow flame. Keep stirring.

5. When the moisture dries up, the gram turns pink and the fat separates, add the sugar.

6. Stir and keep sprinkling milk over.

7. When the sugar dissolves and the mixture becomes thick and semi solid, remove it from the fire.

8. Spread down evenly on a greased metal tray, in a $1 - 1\frac{1}{2}''$ thick layer.

9. Decorate with cardamoms, dry fruits and silver sheets.

10. Cut in to desired shapes. The burfi can also be set in paper cups.

Makes about 30 pieces.

QUICK DANEDAR BURFI

Requirements:

1 tin (400 gms)	**condensed milk**
300 gms grated	**cottage cheese**

For decoration : $\frac{1}{2}$ teaspoon cardamom powder, 2 tablespoons chopped almonds and pistas, 2 silver sheets

Steps

1. Mix condensed milk and cottage cheese. Cook in a karahi on a medium to slow flame. Keep stirring.

2. When the mixture starts thickening, reduce the flame. When it leaves the sides of the karahi and is semisolid, remove from the fire.

3. Spread it in a $1\frac{1}{2}''$ thick layer on a greased surface.

4. Sprinkle cardamom powder and dry fruits. Decorate with the silver sheets.

5. Cut into squares and store in the refrigerator.

Makes 15-20 pieces.

RAWA BURFI

Requirements

125 gms	**ghee**
250 gms	**semolina**
1 cup	**water**
250 gms	**sugar**
50 gms	**dry coconut (grated)**

For decoration : $\frac{1}{2}$ teaspoon cardamom powder, 1 tablespoon *chironji*

Steps

1. Heat ghee in a karahi. Add the semolina and fry on a slow flame till pink in colour. Remove from the fire.

2. Boil the water and sugar. Prepare a $2\frac{1}{2}$ string syrup.

3. Add the hot syrup to the fried semolina and mix well. Also add the coconut and half the cardamom.

4. Spread the mixture on a greased metal tray. Press down evenly.

5. Sprinkle chironji and remaining cardamom over.

6. Cut into square or diamond shaped burfies, using a greased sharp knife.

Makes about 20 pieces.

SHRIKHAND BURFI

Requirements

1 kg	**fresh thick curd**
100 gms	**khoya**
350 gms	**sugar**
4-6 drops	**yellow or orange colour**
$\frac{1}{2}$ teaspoon	**cardamom powder**
25 gms	**chironji**

For decoration : 1 silver sheet

Steps

1. Hang curd in a muslin cloth for 6-8 hours, till all the water is removed. Take out the thick curd called 'chakka' from the muslin cloth.

2. Mix it with the sugar and mashed khoya.

3. Cook the mixture in a karahi on a medium to slow flame. Keep stirring.

4. When the mixture thickens and leaves the sides of the karahi, remove it from the fire.

5. Spread the mixture on a greased surface. Sprinkle cardamom powder and chironji over. Decorate with the silver sheet and cut it in to diamond shapes.

Makes 15-20 pieces.

TIL MAWA BURFI

Requirements

200 gms	**white sesame**
200 gms	**khoya**
300 gms	**powdered sugar**
25 gms	**cashew nuts (chopped)**

For decoration : $\frac{1}{2}$ teaspoon cardamom powder, 2 silver sheets

Steps

1. Roast the sesame in a dry karahi on a slow flame. Keep stirring. When it is light, fluffy and pink in colour, remove it from the fire.

2. When cold, crush it lightly but evenly, in a grinder.

3. Mash the khoya and roast it to a light pink colour on a slow flame.

4. Mix together the sesame khoya, sugar and chopped cashew. Keep it aside for 10 minutes.

5. Press the mixture evenly on a greased surface, in a $1\frac{1}{2}$" thick layer. Let it cool.

6. Decorate it with cardamoms and silver sheets. Cut into square or rectangular burfies, using a sharp greased knife.

Makes about 25 pieces.

TIL GUR BURFI

Requirements

250 gms	**white sesame**
200 gms	**molasses**
1/2 cup	**water**

For decoration : 2 tablespoons dry coconut grated, $\frac{1}{2}$ teaspoon cardamom powder.

Steps

1. Roast sesame in a dry karahi on a slow flame. Keep stirring. When it is light, fluffy and pink in colour, remove it from the fire.

2. Crush the sesame lightly in a grinder.

3. Crush the molasses. Add water and boil on a medium to slow flame to prepare a $2\frac{1}{2}$ string syrup.

4. Mix the hot syrup and sesame thoroughly.

5. Immediately spread it on a greased surface. Even it with a wet palm.

6. Sprinkle cardamom and coconut over.

7. Cut into square shaped burfies.

Makes 15 pieces.

Variations

1. Sugar may be used in place of the molasses.

2. Round laddus can be prepared with the same burfi mixture. Shape them with moist palms.

3. Whole roasted sesame may be used without crushing.

4. These burfies and laddus can be stored for a month or so without fear of spoiling.

Malai Chop,
Tricolour Burfi and
Kaju Rolls

Shrikhand

Kesari Boondi Laddu, Boondi Laddu (back ground Imarti, Patisa, Burfis)

GULAB JAMUNS

GULAB JAMUN

Requirements

500 gms	**khoya**
60-65 gms	**refined flour**
750 gms	**ghee for deep frying.**
750 gms	**sugar**
5-6 cups	**water**
$\frac{1}{4}$ teaspoon	**cardamom powder**
6-8 threads	**saffron dissolved in a little hot water**
6 large	**(brown) cardamoms**

Steps

1. Grate or mash the khoya. Add the flour and prepare a soft dough. If required, add a tablespoon of water.

2. Heat ghee in a karahi, till it fumes, cool it till it is warm.

3. Boil the sugar and water. Prepare a $1\frac{1}{2}$ string syrup. Add cardamom powder and saffron water.

4. Make a small ball out of the dough and, fry it on a slow to medium flame, to a deep brown colour. Immerse it in syrup. Test for perfection (see note).

5. Prepare the rest of the balls, each the size of a small lemon. Fill a grain of brown cardamom in each ball.

6. Fry all the gulab jamuns in batches of 8-10, on a slow to medium fire. Drain and put them in syrup.

   Buy the khoya specially for gulab jamuns known as fatless or Dab ka khoya.

Makes about 50-55 Gulab Jamuns.

Note: Test for perfection

Fry and test one gulab jamun for Perfection. A perfect gulab jamun should:

i) Absorb syrup in 2- 3 minutes. It should immerse in the syrup and float.

ii) Swell and enlarge mainly in syrup and not much during frying.

iii) Be firm, soft and with out any crease or crack.

Contd. . . .

Look for the following defects and correct accordingly.

i)   After putting it in syrup, if the gulab jamun creases, it indicates that the fat content of the dough is less. Add 2-3 teaspoons of ghee to the dough.

ii) If after putting in syrup, a solid ball remains in the centre, it indicates that there is too much of flour in the dough.

Add 2-3 teaspoons of ghee to the dough.

iii) After putting it in syrup if the gulab jamun breaks and spreads or is too soft, it indicates that there is too much fat in the dough. Rub the dough on a blotting paper or dry cloth. Add 2-3 teaspoons of flour to the dough.

Varieties:

KALA JAMUNS

In place of 500 gms khoya, use a mixture of 350 gms khoya and 150 gms cottage cheese. Grate and mix them. Follow the normal recipe.

DECORATIVE GULAB JAMUNS

Shape the gulab jamuns in oblong, mini balls, pyramid, rectangle, square, heart or diamond shapes. Deep fry them and then, put them in syrup. Drain and arrange in paper cups. Decorate with cream icing on top.

CREAM ICING

Beat 1/2 cup fresh cream and 1 tablespoon powdered sugar in a bowl, kept over ice cubes. Beat till it becomes thick and of icing consistency. Fill in a icing bag with star nozzle. Press flowers on gulab jamuns. For coloured flowers mix few drops of any colour in to the icing.

Prepare large oblong gulab jamuns. Cut them in slices and serve.

SANDWICHED GULAB JAMUNS

Fry oval or round but slightly flattened gulab jamuns using 3 table spoons of khoya mixture Soak them thoroughly in syrup. When cold, slit them into two. Spread a layer of white or coloured cottage cheese icing or Khoya icing. Sandwich together with the same mixture.

When each slice is decorated and arranged separately, they are called Gulab jamun chops.

Contd. . . . .

COTTAGE CHEESE ICING

Finely mash 3 tablespoons cottage cheese with a table spoon of milk and a tablespoon of powdered sugar. Mix a drop of Vanilla essence. Add colour for coloured icing. Fill the mixture in an icing bag with a star nozzle. Use this mixture for sandwiching gulab jamun, for icing down flowers, or making borders on them.

KHOYA ICING

Smoothly mash 3 tablespoons of khoya and a table spoon of powdered sugar. If the mixture is hard add a tea spoon of milk. Add colour and essence if required. Use for decorations and icing as done with cream or cheese icing.

MAWA BATI

Make balls the size of walnuts. Fill them with a teaspoon of chopped dry fruits like cashew, almond chironji and raising. Add a tablespoon of sugar and 10-12 saffron flakes to the dry fruits before filling. Keep fried mawa baties in syrup till they are served. Serve them hot by keeping the container in hot water.

KHOYE KI JALEBI

Prepare the usual gulab jamun khoya mixture. Take 3-4 tablespoons of mixture, roll into a thin half centimetre long roll. Arrange it in a spiral like a jalebi. Carefully slip it into hot ghee and fry it to a deep brown. Drain and soak in normal syrup. When the syrup has been absorbed thoroughly, remove the jalebis and serve.

MILK POWDER GULAB JAMUN

Requirements:

350 gms	**sugar**
$1\frac{1}{2}$ cups	**water**
200 gms	**milk powder**
30 gms	**refined flour**
	$\frac{1}{8}$ **teaspoon soda bicarbonate**
1 tablespoon	**pure ghee,**
	a little milk for kneading
400 gms	**ghee for frying**
	2-3 cardamoms, peeled
4-6 drops	**rose essence**

Steps

1. Boil the sugar and water. Prepare a $1\frac{1}{2}$ string syryp. Add rose essence.

2. Sieve flour, milk power and soda bicarbonate together.

3. Rub 1 tablespoon ghee in the mixture.

4. Gradually add milk and knead in to a pliable dough.

5. Heat ghee in a karahi. Remove from heat and cool it till it becomes warm. Keep the karahi back on a slow flame.

6. Prepare 20 balls of the mixture . Fill a seed or two of cardamom in each ball.

7. Deep fry balls in batches of 5-6 at a time. When golden brown, drain and remove.

8. Put the fried gulab jamuns in syrup. Serve after an hour.

Makes 20 Gulab Jamuns.

HALWA

MOONG DAL HALWA

Requirements

500 gms	**green gram**
650 gms	**ghee**
450 gms	**sugar**
1 litre	**milk**
1/2 teaspoon	**cardamom powder**
8 - 10 threads	**saffron soaked in 2 tablespoons hot water**
50 gms	**cashew nuts**
25 gms	**almonds**

For decoration : 1 silver sheet

Steps

1. Soak gram overnight. Wash, rub and remove the green skin. Drain and grind it on a stone, using as little water as possible.

2. Heat 500 gms of ghee in a karahi. Add the ground paste in ghee and fry on a medium to slow flame for 45-60 minutes.

3. When it turns pink in colour, dries and the ghee separates, add sugar and milk,

4. Cook the mixture on a slow flame. Keep stirring.

5. When the mixture dries up again, add the remaining ghee. Fry for 3-4 minutes. Add half the chopped dry fruits and saffron water.

6. Remove from the fire. Decorate with remaining dry fruits, caradamom and the silver sheet.

Makes about 1.5 kg Halwa.

GAJAR HALWA

Requirements

2 Kg	carrots
2 litres	milk
450 gms	sugar
100 gms	ghee
200 gms	khoya
1/2 teaspoon	cardamom powder
75 gms	chopped dry fruits like cashews, and almonds.

For decoration : silver sheets

Steps

1. Wash, peel and grate the carrots.

2. Mix the milk and grated carrots. Cook on a medium flame, in a karahi, stirring occasionally. After 45-60 minutes, the mixture will dry up.

3. Add sugar and let the mixture cook on a slow flame, till it dries up once more.

4. Add ghee and fry thoroughly.

5. Add the mashed khoya. Cook for 5-7 minutes. Remove from the fire.

6. Mix in cardamom and dry fruits. Decorate with the silver sheets.

Makes about 2 kg Halwa.

SOOJI HALWA

Requirements

1 litre	**water**
250 gms	**sugar**
200 gms	**ghee**
500 gms	**semolina**
1/2 teaspoon	**cardamom powder**
70 gms	**chopped dry fruits like cashews, raisins, almonds, chironji etc.**

For decoration : 1 silver sheet

Steps

1. Boil the water and sugar. Keep aside.

2. Heat ghee in a karahi. Add semolina and fry to a pink colour on a medium to slow flame.

3. When the ghee separates, add sugar water. Cover and cook on a slow flame for 1-2 minutes.

4. Stir and mixture half the cardamom and dry fruits.

5. Decorate with the remaining dry fruits and the silver sheet.

Makes about 1.75 Kg Halwa.

Variation : Replace semolina with wheat flour to make atte ka halwa in the same way.

JALEBIS

JALEBI

Requirements

250 gms	**refined flour**
25 gms	**gramflour**
1 tablespoon	**refined oil**
1 cup	**curds**
$1\frac{1}{2}$ cups	**water**
350 gms	**sugar**
2 cups	**water**
2-3 pinches	**yellow colour**
4-6 threads	**saffron soaked in 2 tablespoons hot milk**
500 gms	**ghee for deep frying**

Steps

1 Mix together the flours, oil and curds. Add water to make a medium thick paste. Cover and keep overnight for fermentation.

2 Prepare a two string syrup with the sugar and water. Add colour and saffron milk.

3 Heat ghee in a frying pan.

4 Beat the mixture well. Fill in a thick plastic bag. Cut a small hole at one of the bottom corner.

5 Squeeze out the batter by pressing the plastic bag into the hot ghee . Drop medium sized whirls in a continuous flow begining from outer circle and ending in the centre. This will give better shape to the jalebies.

6 Fry them crisp on both the sides. Carefully turn them with an iron needle or stick to prevent them from breaking. Drain and drop in the syrup.

7 In five minutes the jalebies will be thoroughly soaked. Drain and serve hot.

Makes about 40 Jalebis.

IMARTI

Requirements

250 gms	**white gram (washed)**
350 gms	**sugar**
$1\frac{1}{2}$ cups	**water**
2-3 pinches	**orange colour (dry)**
500 gms	**ghee for deep frying**

Piece of thick cloth with a small hole in the centre which is finished with button - hole stitch or an imarti nozzle.

Steps

1 Soak the gram overnight. Grind it to a fine paste of medium thickness with 1/2 -1 cup water Keep aside for 2 (in summer) to 4 (in winter) hours. No fermentation is required.

2 Boil the sugar and water. Prepare a two string syrup. When it cools, add colour. (Colour can also be added to the gram paste.)

3 Beat the paste till light and fluffy. It should float in water.

4 Heat the ghee in a karahi on a medium flame.

5 Fill the cloth with the grampaste, gather it up and press it to drop a continuous pattern of a flower having a round centre and 7 round petals, in hot ghee. If you are using a nozzle fit it into the button hole of the cloth.

6 Fry imarties crisp. Drain and put them in the syrup. When they are thoroughly soaked, removed them and serve.

Makes around 15-16 Imartis.

Note:

At times, due to overbeating, the gram paste becomes rubber-like instead of light and fluffy. If this is the case, add a little flour and gramflour to improve the texture.

INSTANT JALEBIS

Requirements

200 gms	refined flour
1 teaspoon	fruit salt (e.g. ENO)
1 teaspoon	gramflour
2 teaspoon	curds
1 teaspoon	refined oil
300 gms	sugar
2 cups	water
	a pinch of orange colour or saffron water
	A piping bag with a single hole nozzle or a thick polythene bag.
400 gms	ghee for deep frying

Steps

1 Mix the flour gram flour and fruit salt. Add curds and refined oil.

 Make a thick batter with a little water. Keep for 10 minutes.

2 Prepare a two string syrup with the sugar and water. Add colour or saffron water.

3 Heat ghee in a frying pan.

4 Fill the bag with batter. If you are using a polythene bag, make a small hole at one bottom corner.

5 Press out round whirls into the hot ghee, working closely from out side to the centre of the whirl. Fry them golden crisp.

 Turn with an iron needle, stick or skewer.

6 Drain and slip them into the syrup. In two minutes they will be throughly soaked. Drain and serve.

Makes 30-35 Jalebis

Note:

Instant jalebies should be made and served immediately as they become soggy if kept too long.

LADDUS

BESAN LADDU

Requirements

150 gms	**ghee or fat**
350 gms	**gram flour**
175 gms	**sugar powder**
1 teaspoon	**cardamom powder**
6-8 flakes	**saffron dissolved in a tablespoon of hot milk.**

Steps

1. Heat ghee in a karahi.
2. Add gramflour and cook on a slow flame, stirring all the time.
3. When the flour changes colour and the ghee separates, remove it from the fire. Let it cool.
4. Rub saffron milk in the flour. Add powdered sugar and cardamom.
5. Prepare even sized laddus.

Makes about 20-25 Laddus.

BOONDI LADDU

Requirements

500 gms	**gram flour (slightly coarse variety)**
1 litre	**water or milk**
750 gms	**ghee for deep frying**
750 gms	**sugar**
$3\frac{1}{2}$	**cups water**
10-12 drops	**orange colour**
10-12 flakes	**saffron soaked in a little water**
50 gms	**chopped cashewnuts**
50 gms	**raisings**
10 cardamoms	**peeled**

A boondi strainer or fryer of medium sized holes.
(available in different numbers depending upon the size of holes)

Steps

1. Prepare a thin batter with gramflour and water or milk

2. Heat ghee in a karahi.

3. Fill the fryer or strainer with the batter up to the half. Positioned it over karahi and drain boondis in hot ghee by hitting the strainer on the sides of karahi, lifting up then again hitting.

   This process should be finished very quickly.

4. Fry them to golden colour, drain and remove. Use up all the batter.

5. Prepare a sugar syrup of $1\frac{1}{2}$ thread consistency, by boiling the sugar and water.

6. Add saffron water and colour to the syrup.

7. Mix the boondies, syrup, dry fruits and cardamom.

8. After 10 minutes sprinkle over a little hot water, cover and keep for half an hour.

9. Prepare round balls (laddus) with moist hands.

Makes about 50-55 Laddus.

Note: When laddus are to be stored for a longer period use a two string syrup to make them.

Cond. . . .

Variations:

MOTICHUR LADDUS

They are made with very fine pearl like boondi made with a fine strainer. The syrup made for these laddus is also thin with no string consistency. Some times, motichur boondies are made from green gramflour instead of gramflour.

MULTI COLOURED BOONDI LADDU

Different edible colours like red, green, orange, yellow are used to make a coloured syrup. Boondies soaked in this will vary in colour.

Laddus can be made with these multi-coloured boondies.

MOTI PAK

Moti pak is a variation in shape. Instead of making motichur laddus, the mixture is set like a burfi and arranged in paper cups. The top is decorated with dry fruits like cashew, almond, pista, char magaz and chironji. Cardamom powder and silver sheets may also be used for decoration.

LADDU CHURMA

Requirements

500 gms	semolina
70 gms	ghee.
1 cup	milk.
250 gms	khoya.
350 gms	powdered sugar.
500 gms	ghee for frying.
8-10 strands	saffron soaked in a little hot milk
1/2 tea spoon	cardamom powder
70 grams	mixed chopped dry fruits like cashew, almond, chironji.

Steps:

1. Rub 70 gms ghee into the semolina.

2 Sprinkle milk over and knead roughly to prepare 6-7 flat, tight-balls.

3 Heat ghee in a karahi and fry semolina balls golden crisp. Fry in batches on a medium to slow flame. Drain and remove. Let them cool.

4 Mash and roast khoya to a light pink, in a karahi.

5 Break up semolina balls and mash it into fine grains. Pass through a sieve.

6 Mix together sifted semolina, powdered sugar, dry fruits, cardamom,khoya, saffron water and 4 tablespoons ghee. Use the ghee that remains from frying.

7 Mix all the ingredients well and shape into round balls or laddus.

Makes about 40 Laddus.

SEMOLINA LADDU

Requirements

500 gms	**semolina**
225 gms	**ghee**
100 gms	**khoya**
250 gms	**sugar**
1 cup	**water**
50 gms	**chopped dry fruit mix like cashew, almond, chironji.**
1/2 teaspoon	**cardamom powder**

Steps

1 Fry semolina in ghee, in a karahi to a pink colour on a medium to slow flame.

2 Mash and roast the khoya lightly.

3 Prepare a 2 string syrup with the sugar and water.

4 Mix together all the ingredients. Keep covered for 15 minutes.

5 Shape the mixture into round balls or laddus with moist hands.

Makes about 30-35 Laddus.

KHOYE KE LADDU

Requirements

500 gms	**fresh granulated khoya**
200 gms	**powdered sugar**
6-8	**cardamoms, powdered**
6-8 drops	**rose essence**

For decoration : 8-10 flakes saffron soaked in a teaspoon of water, 10 gms chopped pista, 2 Silver sheets

Steps:

1. Grate khoya lightly.

2. Mix the sugar, cardamom and essence into the khoya. Keep aside for 10-15 minutes in winter or in the refrigerater for 20 minutes in summer.

3. Rub and roll the mixture into 25 balls or laddus.

4. Arrange them in paper cups.

5. Decorate with saffron flakes, pista and bits of the silver sheets.

6. To store refrigerate specially in summer.

Makes 25 Laddus.

* Granulated khoya is a type of khoya, made out of milk to which little tartaric acid is added during khoya making process.

SONTH KE LADDU

Requirements

500 gms	good quality wheat flour
300 gms	ghee
250 gms	sugar
1 cup	water
$\frac{1}{2}$ teaspoon	cardamom powder
$\frac{1}{2}$ tablespoon	dry ginger powder
100 gms	chopped dry fruits like cashew nuts, almonds, *chironji* and raisins.

Steps

1. Fry wheat flour in the ghee, in a karahi. Fry to a light brown on a medium to slow flame.

2. Prepare a two string syrup with the sugar and water.

3. Mix together all the ingredients.

4. Prepare round laddus out of the mixture.

Makes about 30-35 Laddus.

PANEER LADDU

Requirements

500 gms	**fresh cottage cheese**
200 gms	**powdered sugar**
1 tablespoon	**refined flour**
$\frac{1}{2}$ teaspoon	**cardamom powder**
$\frac{1}{4}$ teaspoon	**rose essence**
125 gms	**desiccated coconut**

Steps

1. Mash or grind the cottage cheese to a fine paste.

2. Mix it together with the sugar and flour.

3. Cook in a heavy bottomed pan or karahi, on a medium flame.

4. Stirring continuously, cook for 8-12 minutes. When the mixture becomes thick and dries up, remove it from the fire.

5. Add the cradamom and essence. Shape 25-30 balls or laddus out of mixture.

6. Spread the desiccated coconut on a paper and roll the laddus on it.

7. Refrigerate.

Makes 25-30 Laddus.

URD DAL LADDU

Requirements

500 gms	**white gram flour**
250 gms	**ghee or fat**
300 gms	**powdered sugar**
1/2 teaspoon	**nutmeg powder**
or 6-8 teaspoon	**threads of saffron dissolved in a little hot milk.**
1/2 teaspoon	**cardamom powder**

For decoration : 2-3 silver sheets

Steps

1. Heat ghee in a karahi. Add flour and fry on a medium to slow flame till golden yellow in colour. Remove from the fire, turn onto a plate and let it cool.

2. When it is just warm, add all the other ingredients. Mix well.

3. Moisten the palms with milk and prepare round laddus of required size.

4. Decorate each laddu with bits of silver.

Makes 25-30 Laddus.

MAGAJ LADDU

Requirements

500 gms	**gramflour (a slightly coarse variety)**
30 gms	**ghee**
1/2 cup	**milk**
300 gms	**ghee**
350 gms	**powdered sugar**
1/2 teaspoon	**cardamom powder**

For decoration : 2-3 silver sheets.

Steps

1. Rub the 30 gms ghee in to the gramflour. Sprinkle milk over, mix well and keep for half an hour.

2. Rub the mixture to the consistency of even crumbs. This is called Magaj.

3. Heat ghee in a karahi. Add magaj and fry to a golden brown colour, on a medium to slow flame.

4. Remove from the fire. Turn on to a plate and let it cool.

5. Add the sugar and cardamom. Mix well and prepare balls with palms moistered with milk.

6. Decorate each laddu with bits of silver sheet.

Makes around 22-26 Laddus.

PINNIS

Rasgullas

Coconut Burfi, Amriti, Pinni, Petha

URD KI PINNI

Requirements

250 gms	white gram (without skin)
300 gms	ghee
100 gms	khoya
300 gms	powdered sugar
50 gms	mixed and chopped dry fruits like cashew, almond

For decoration : 6-8 cardamom powdered, $\frac{1}{2}$ cup milk, 25 gms almonds

Steps

1. Soak the gram for 4-6 hours. Wash, drain and grind it to a thick, fine paste using as little water as possible.

2. Heat ghee in a karahi. Add the ground paste and cook on a medium flame, stirring frequently.

3. When the paste dries up, is light brown and the ghee separates, remove it from the fire. Spread on a plate. Let it cool.

4. Roast khoya in the same karahi to a light pink colour.

5. Mix together the gram, khoya, sugar, dry fruits and cardamom. Sprinkle over little milk, rub the mixture and make pinnis by pressing a fist full of mixture tightly together. The finger marks should be visible on the pinni.

6. Decorate an almond on each pinni.

Makes about 25 Pinnis.

Variation:

Replace white gram with green gram and make pinnis in exactly the same way.

BESAN KI PINNI

Requirements

150 gms	khoya
250 gms	pure ghee
250 gms	coarse gramflour
300 gms	powdered sugar
50 gms	chopped dry fruits like cashews almonds

For decoration : 1/2 cup milk, 1/2 teaspoon cardmom powder, 20 gms cashew

Steps:

1. Mash the khoya and roast to a light pink colour.

2. Heat the ghee in a karahi. Add the gramflour and fry on a slow fire to a light brown colour. Keep stirring.

3. Turn on to the khoya and let the mixture cool.

4. Add the sugar, dry fruits and cardamom. Mix well.

5. Sprinkle milk if required and prepare pinnis by pressing a fist-full of mixture together. Decorate a cashew on each pinni.

Makes 25 Pinnis.

ATTE KI PINNI

Requirements

250 gms	**ghee**
250 gms	**wheatflour**
250 gms	**powdered sugar**
1/2 cup	**milk**
4-6	**cardamoms powdered**

For decoration : 20 gms cashews or almonds.

Steps

1. Heat ghee in a karahi. Add the wheaflour. Fry on a slow flame stirring all the time.

2. When it turns brown in colour and is aromatic, remove it from the fire. Turn in to a plate and let it cool.

3. When it is only slightly warm, add the sugar and cardamom.

4. Sprinkle milk and Make pinnis. Decorate with dry fruit.

Makes 25 Pinnis

RASGULLAS

RASGUELAS

RASGULLA

Requirements

1 litre	**pure cow's milk**
6-8 grams	**tartary or lemon juice**
10 grms	**refined flour**
	a pinch of baking powder
2 cups	**sugar**
5 cups	**water**
1/8 tea spoon	**rose essence**
1 tablespoon	**milk**

Steps

1. Boil milk and keep aside for 4-6 hours. Remove the top cream or malai.

2. Boil the milk again. Dissolve tartary in 2 tablespoons of water and gradually add to the boiling milk till it curdles.

3. Pour curdled milk into a muslin cloth, tie and dip into cold water for 5-7 minutes.

4. Hang up the cloth for 2 hours to remove the water completely.

5. Rub the cottage cheese with palm and fingers (for 10 minutes) till it is soft and smooth. Add the refined flour and baking powder. Rub again.

6. Prepare 12 balls of the mixture.

7. Boil the sugar and water in a deep pan or small pressure cooker. Add milk to cut the scum. Remove the scum by straining the syrup. Turn again into the same utensil. Keep boiling.

8. Add the cheese balls and keep boiling on a high flame.

9. Maintain the consistency of the boiling syrup by adding a spoonful of water at frequent intervals.

10. Boil for 15 minutes on a high flame and five minutes on a slow flame.

11. Remove from the fire. Let the rasgullas cool for 4 hours before serving. Add rose essence.

Variations

COLOURED RASGULLAS

Add a few drops of any colour (yellow, red, orange, green) to the cottage cheese mixture and get various coloured rasgullas.

VARIETY IN SHAPES

Shape rasgullas in different shapes oblongs, cylindrical rectangles or triangles.

RASGULLA BASED DECORATIVE SWEETS

BASIC RECIPE OF RASGULLA TO BE USED IN MAKING DECORATIVE SWEETS

Requirements

1 litre	**cow's milk**
1 litre	**buffalo's milk**
12-15 grams	**tartary dissolved in 1/2 cup of water**
50 grams	**refined flour**
1.2 kg	**sugar**
13 cups	**water (2.5 litres)**
$^1/_4$ cup	**milk**
	a pinch of Sodium Hydrosulphite (to bleach rasgulla to a white colour).
2	**reethas (used in making shampoo) crushed and boiled in 1 cup water.**

Steps

1. Boil both the milks separately. When cold, refrigerate the buffalo milk for 4-6 hours, Remove cream from both the milks and mix together.

2. Boil the milk and gradually add tartary water to curdle the milk.

3. Separate the cheese from the milk and pour cold water on it. Hang it in a muslin cloth for 2-4 hours to remove all the water. The cheese should be soft.

4. Rub the cheese on a cloth till light and fluffy. Mix in the flour and baking powder and rub again.

5. Boil the sugar and water. Add milk to separate the scum. Strain the syrus and keep aside half of it. Add sodium Hydrosulphite to the remaining and boil it to a 2 string thick consistency. Keep aside.

6. Boil the thin syrup in a broad karahi. Prepare required sized and shaped rasgullas and slip in to the boiling syrup.

7. Every once in a while sprinkle reetha water on boiling Rasgullas. When the syrup thickens sprinkle a little cold water. Repeat this process thrice.

8. Boil for 20-25 minutes on a high to medium flame. When the Rasgullas start floating half in and half out of the syrup, remove from the fire.

9. Add the thick syrup. Keep for 4-6 hours before decorating.

HEMKUND

Requirements

6 oblong	**rasgullas approximately** $3'' \times 1\frac{1}{2} \times 1''$
75 gms	**khoya**
50 gms	**cottage cheese**
50 gms	**powdered sugar**
1/4 teaspoon	**rose essence**
2 tablespoons	**khoya crumbs (roasted and mashed khoya)**

For decoration : 2 silver sheets 6-8 flakes saffron soaked in a tablespoon of hot water

Steps

1. Mix khoya, cheese essence and sugar. Rub and knead into a dough. Roll out thinly on a plastic sheet. Cut into rectangles slightly bigger to cover each Rasgulla completely. Place a Rasgulla on a sheet, roll, seal and smoothen the cover

2. Roll and cover all the Rasgullas into these sheets. Roll in khoya crumbs.

3. Decorate with silver bits and saffron flakes. Refrigerate.

MALAI CHOP

Requirements

6 triangle	**shaped large Rasgullas.**
1 cup	**thick chilled cream from top of the milk.**
1 tablespoon	**powdered sugar**
6-8 flakes	**saffron in a table spoon of hot water**

For decoration : 1/4 teaspoon rose essence, 1 tablespoon chopped pista.

Steps

1. Slit each Rasgulla triangle in to two.

2. Decorate each triangle (on the cut side) with a layer of cream, a sprinkle of sugar, a touch of essence, saffron flakes and pista. Chill before serving.

Note:

When another Rasgulla trangle is placed on top the sweet is called a Malai sandwich.

VASANT MADHURI

Requirements

	6	**Heart Shaped large Rasgullas with yellow coloured centre**
For the icing	150 gms	**khoya**
	75 gms	**cottage cheese**
	100 gms	**sugar, powdered**
	$^1/_4$ teaspoon	**rose essence**
	1–2 teaspoon	**milk if required**

To make 6 Large heart shaped Rasgullas with yellow colour in the centre, add few drops of yellow colour to one fourth of the cheese mixture Prepare yellow balls the size of small lemon and fill in the centre of heart shape Follow the rest of the normal recipe. When you will slit them there will be a yellow round in the centre.

Steps

1. Prepare Khoya cheese icing by mashing smoothly the khoya and cheese. Rub in the sugar and essence. If the icing is too thick to spread add little milk.

2. Slit each Rasgulla.

3. Decorate each piece with a border of flowery icing, with an icing gun.

4. Refrigerate and serve

Variations

ROSO MADHURI
Cover oblong Rasgullas with icing mixture. Decorate with chopped pistas.

PAKEEZA
Slit and fill oblong rasgullas with icing mixture. Arrange little icing on top. Shape it slanting on both the sides with a knife. Decorate with a silver sheet, saffron and chopped pistas.

Contd. . . . . .

DIL BAHAR

Prepare tiny Rasgullas the size of cherries. Prepare khoya cheese icing and divide in to lemon sized balls Stuff the Rasgullas in these balls. Spread khoya crumbs and roll in these balls in them.

RAJ BHOG

Prepare Rasgullas by normal method. But while makiing cheese balls stuff them with a cherry size ball of mashed khoya to which little yellow colour is added.

RASMALAI

Requirements

12	Rasgullas
1 litre	pure buffalo milk
75 gms	sugar

For decoration : $^1/_2$ silver sheet, 4-6 pistas chopped, 4 cardamoms powdered.

Steps

1. Boil milk till reduced to 700 ml.

2. Add sugar and boil for 5 minutes.

3. Drain excess syrup from the Rasgullas and add to the boiling milk. Keep boiling on a slow flame till the Rasgullas are soft and milk thickens further.

4. Remove from the fire. Cool, then refrigerate. Decorate with cardamoms, pistas and silver sheet.

OTHER SWEETS

Laddus – (top to bottom) Kesari, Motichur, Magal, Boondi, Semolina

Patisa, Ladoo, Pedda and a variety of Burfis

Small Rasgullas and Gulabjamuns commonly known as Rasberries

ANARSA

Requirements

500 gms	rice
350 gms	powdered sugar
50 ml	milk
100 gms	poppy seeds
500 gms	ghee or fat

Steps

1. Soak the rice in water for three days. Change the water everyday.

2. On the fourth day, drain water. Spread the rice on a dry cloth to remove excess moisture.

3. Grind the rice very finely and sieve.

4. Mix the rice and sugar powder. Press into tight balls. Keep aside for four to six hours.

5. Sprinkle a little milk and knead the rice and sugar into a tight dough.

6. Prepare small walnut sized balls. Sprinkle a few poppy seeds on a plastic sheet. Use finger tips to press and rotate the ball on poppy seeds. Spread into a thin circle.

7. Meanwhile, heat two-three serving spoons ghee in a frying pan. Carefully slip an anarsa into the ghee with poppy seeds side up.

8. Shallow fry to a golden brown colour on a medium flame. Drain and remove. Fry all the anarsas in this way.

9. Store when cold and crisp.

Instructions

1. While making dough sprinkle milk carefully. Otherwise, the dough will become soft due to the sugar separating from the water.

2. If a fine network does not appear on the anarsa while frying, it indicates that the circles are either too thick or the dough is too hard or too soft. Correct it accordingly, before frying.

3. If anarsas are not crisp, it indicates that the circles are too thick or are under fried.

Makes around 55-60 Anarsas.

BALUSHAHI

Requirements

500 gms	**refined flour**
3/4 teaspoon	**soda bicarbonate**
125 gms	**fat or ghee**
2-3 tablespoons	**curds**
500 gms	**sugar**
2 cups	**water**
750 gms	**ghee for deep frying**
	Cold water for kneading

For decoration : 10 gms chopped pista, 6 -8 cardamoms, powdered. A few silver sheets.

Steps

1. Sieve flour and soda bicarbonate together, twice.

2. Rub the 125 gms ghee into the flour lightly. Mix in curds.

3. Add cold water gradually and prepare a very tight dough. Cover with a dry cloth.

4. Boil together the sugar and water. Prepare a 2½ string syrup.

5. For frying, heat ghee in a karahi. Remove from heat and cool to a luke-warm stage. Again keep on a slow flame.

6. Divide the dough into thirty balls. Flatten them slightly and press each with the thumb, at the centre.

7. Deep fry them on a slow flame till half done on both the sides.

8. Fry them to a golden brown on medium flame.

9. When cold, dip them in the sugar syrup.

10. Arrange on a tray and decorate with chopped pista, cardamom powder and silver sheets.

Makes 30 Balushahis.

CHANDRAKALA

Requirements

For syrup:	500 gms	**sugar**
	2 cups	**water**
	2 crushed	**cardamoms**
	4 drops	**orange colour**
For filling:	250 gms	**khoya**
	100 gms	**cashew nuts**
	50 gms	**almonds**
	50 gms	**chironji**
	225 gms	**powdered sugar**
	1/4 teaspoon	**nutmeg powder or saffron**
	1/4 teaspoon	**cardamom powder**
For covering:	500 gms	**refined flour**
	75 gms	**ghee**
		a pinch of salt
		water for kneading
	750 gms	**ghee for deep frying**

For decoration : 3 silver sheets

Steps

1. Prepare a two string syrup by boiling the sugar and water. When it cools, add the orange colour and crushed cardamoms.

2. To prepare the filling, mash the khoya and roast it in a karahi, to a light pink colour on a medium to slow flame. When the khoya is warm add all the chopped dry fruits, sugar, nutmeg and cardamom.

3. To make the covering, sift the flour and salt. Rub the 75 gms ghee into it. Add water gradually and knead into a tight dough. In summer, cover it with a moist cloth.

4. Make a ball of the size of a lemon and roll it in to a circle of 2"-3" diametre. Use up all the dough this way. Keep covered with a moist cloth.

Contd. . . .

5. Place 2 teaspoons full of filling in the centre of a cricle, moisten the circumference and cover with an another circle. Press along the circumference. Cut and secure the circular edges with a cutter or twist it inside at regular intervals forming a pattern. Prepare all the *chandrakalas* this way.

6. Heat ghee in a large karahi. Deep fry *chandrakalas* on medium flame, to a golden yellow colour.

7. Dip them in the sugar syrup in batches. Keep each batch in the syrup for five minutes, then drain and arrange in a plate. Decorate each one with bits of the silver sheet

Makes 20-25 pieces.

CHIKKI

PEANUT CHIKKI

Requirements

250 gms	**roasted peanuts**
200 gms	**molasses**
$\frac{1}{2}$ cup	**water**

Steps

1. Remove skin or husk from the roasted peanuts.

2. Crush the peanuts very coarsely. This is optional. Chikki can also be made with whole peanuts.

3. Crush the jaggery. Add water and prepare a $2\frac{1}{2}$ string syrup, on a medium to slow flame.

4. Add peanuts to the syrup and immediately pour on to a greased metal tray. The layer should be 1-2" thick.

5. Cut into pieces with a greased sharp knife. Store when cold.

Makes about 15 pieces.

Note — Round or square slabs of chikkies can also be prepared using different shaped tins.

CHIROTE

Requirements

500 gms	**refined flour**
	a pinch of salt
70 gms	**ghee**
3 tablespoons	**rice flour**
3 tablespoons	**ghee**
700 gms	**ghee for deep frying**
200 gms	**powdered sugar for dusting on chirotes**

Steps

1. Mix the flour and salt. Rub 70 gms ghee and knead into a tight, pliable dough with cold water. Divide into 21 equal parts.

2. Roll each part in to a paper thin round sheets

3. Cream together 3 tablespoons ghee and rice flour.

4. Divide 21 rounds into 3 sets of 7 sheets each. Place these 7 sheets one over another, brushing top of each with rice-ghee mixture.

5. Tightly roll together this heap of 7 sheets into a roll. cut the roll in to 15 slices. Lightly roll each slice with a rolling pin. Repeat this process of making chirote with the other two sets also.

6. Heat ghee in a karahi. Deep fry chirotes on a slow to medium flame in batches. Fry to a golden pink colour. Drain and let them cool.

7. When still warm, sprinkle powdered sugar on each chirote. When cold, store them in an airtight container.

Makes 45 Chirote.

Note: A two-and-a-half string sugar syrup can be brushed on to the chirotes instead of powdered sugar.

GUJIYA

Requirements

For filling :

500 gms	khoya
350 gms	powdered sugar
50 gms	dessicated coconut
25 gms	cashew nuts chopped
25 gms	almonds chopped
25 gms	raisins
$\frac{1}{2}$ teaspoon	cardamom powder
or $\frac{1}{2}$ teaspoon	nutmeg powder.

For outer covering:

500 gms	refined flour
	a pinch of salt
	water for kneading
75 gms	ghee
1 kg	ghee for frying
	a gujiya mould

Steps

1. First prepare the filling. Mash the khoya and roast it in a karahi on a medium flame. When it is pink in colour, remove from the fire and let it cool.

2. Add all the other filling ingredients to the khoya.

3. To prepare the dough for the covering, sieve the flour and salt. Rub the 75 gms, ghee into it. Add the water and knead into a tight dough. Cover it with a moist cloth.

4. Divide dough into balls of the size of small potato. Roll each ball into thin small round of $3^1/_2$ - 4" diametre.

5. Spread a round in the greased gujiya mould. Fill a tablespoon of filling mixture, on one side. Moisten the edges of the round and fold one side of the mould over the other. Remove the excess edges of each round for reuse.

6. Prepare all the gujiyas as explained. Spread on a cloth.

7. Start frying. Heat ghee in a karahi and deep fry them on a medium to slow flame, in batches. When golden yellow in colour, drain and remove.

8. Store in an air-tight container, when cold.

Makes 35-40 gujiyas.

Note— Gujiya edges can also be moulded with fingers or a cutter.

KALAKAND

Requirements

1 litre	**rich buffalo milk**
100 gms	**sugar**
2-3 pinches	**tartaric powder**
1 teaspoon	**cornflour**
6-8 threads	**saffron in a tablespoon of hot water**

For decoration : 4 cardamoms powdered, 4 pistas chopped, 1 silver sheet

Steps

1   Boil milk in a karahi. Add tartaric powder pinch by pinch till the milk curdles slightly. Tiny granules should stick at the back of the spoon.

2   Keep boiling, stirring occasionally. When reduced by half, add the sugar.

3   When the mixture thickens reduce the flame. Keep stirring. When the mixture becomes semi-solid and frothy sprinkle cornflour over. Remove from the fire.

4   Turn the mixture onto a greased tray. Spread in a $1\frac{1}{2}$" thick even layer.

5   Decorate with cardamoms, pista and silver sheet.

6   Cut into squares. Store in the refrigerator.

Makes about 8-10 pieces.

Variations

VARIATION IN FLAVOUR

Differently flavoured kalakand can be made by adding to the kalakand mixture rose, pineapple, orange, lemon, nutmeg, saffron, almond, flavour or cocoa powder.

Contd.....

VARIATION IN COLOUR

Use edible liquid colours like red, yellow, orange, green or chocolate to make differently coloured kalakand.

VARIATION IN USE OF DRY FRUITS

Use various dry fruits (chopped) like walnut, almond, chironji, cashew or even grated chocolate, to cover the kalakand. Set it in paper cups.

VARIATION IN SHAPES

Use different moulds to shape the kalakand.

VARIATION IN TASTE

Use molasses, caramel sugar or honey in place of ordinary sugar.

CASHEW KATLI

Requirements

100 gms	**cashew nuts**
80 gms	**powdered sugar**
1 teaspoon	**corn flour**
1/3 teaspoon	**rose essence**

For decoration : 1 silver sheet

Steps

1. Soak cashew nuts in water, for 1-2 hours.

2. Drain and grind them to a fine paste on a grinding stone, using as little water as possible.

3. Mix together the sugar and cashew paste. Cook in a karahi on a medium flame.

4. When the mixture thickens, reduce the flame and keep stirring.

5. When the mixture becomes thick and comes away from the sides of the pan (it should take 8 minutes), sprinkle cornflour, stir well, and remove from the fire.

6. Immediately, mix in the rose essence and quickly turn onto a greased marble or wooden surface.

7. Quickly, roll thinly with a greased roller. Spread the silver sheet over and cut into diamond shaped katlis.

8. Store in an air-tight container when cold.

Makes 20 katlis.

Variations:

FLAVOURS AND COLOURS

Different essences like saffron, nutmeg, cardamom, pineapple, orange can be used in place of rose essence.

Contd. . . .

To make differently coloured katli use colours like red, orange, lemon, pineapple, green and yellow. Mix the colour into the mixture before spreading it out for rolling.

SHAPES AND FILLINGS

Katlis can be made in different shapes.

Prepare different shapes out of the katli mixture. For tarts and stuffed rolls use fillings like carrot halwa, dry fruits, coconut, sweetened khoya etc.

Roll out katli mixture in to a thin sheet. Spread the filling over it. Roll over the sheet tightly. Cut into $2\frac{1}{2}$" long pieces. These are called cashew rolls.

To prepare cashew tarts, cut out small rounds using cookie moulds. Fill these rounds with filling mixture.

Decorate the fillings top with bits of silver sheet, chopped dry fruits cardamom powder or saffron.

PISTA KATLI

Requirements

100 gms	**pistas**
75 gms	**powdered sugar**
4 drops	**rose essence.**

For decoration : 1/4 teaspoon cardamom powder one silver sheet.

Steps

1   Soak pistas in water for 30 minutes. Drain water and grind to a coarse paste.

2   Mix the pistas and sugar well.

3   Cook in a karahi on a medium to slow flame. Keep stirring.

4   In 7-8 minutes the mixture will thicken and come away from sides of the karahi. Remove it from the fire. Mix in essence.

5   Quickly transfer the mixture on to a greased wooden or marble board.

6   Roll in to a thin square with a greased rolling pin.

7   Sprinkle cardamom over and press down silver sheets over it. Cut it into diamond or square shapes.

Makes 16-18 pieces.

VARIATIONS

In the same manner, prepare almond katli. Replace pista with almonds. Soak and remove the skin before using them.

Cheaper replacement for pistas or almonds are roasted peanuts. Remove the skin from them. Soak them in water, grind coarsely and follow the same method. Use 3-4 drops of almond essence to disguise them as almond katlis.

Different shapes and moulds can be used instead to cut the katli. Arrange the shapes in paper cups and decorate the tops.

Always store katli in an air- tight container. They tend to become dry if kept out in the open.

KOPRA PAK

Requirements

300 gms	**sugar**
3/4 cup	**water**
250 gms	**desiccated coconut**

For decoration: 2 - 3 silver sheets, 1/3 tea spoon cardamom powder.

Steps

1. Boil the sugar and water. Prepare a $2\frac{1}{2}$ string syrup.

2. Immediately, add the coconut. Mix well and spread it out evenly on a greased surface.

3. Decorate with silver sheets and cardamom.

4. Cut in to pieces with a greased sharp knife.

Makes 25-30 pieces.

Variations

Use different colours like red, orange, yellow, green to colour the Kopra Pak. For variety, you can also use different flavours like kesar, pista, nutmeg, vanilla, rose, pineapple, orange.

MYSORE PAK

Requirements

1 kg	**sugar**
4 cups	**water**
250 gms	**fine gramflour**
250 gms	**refined flour**
$1\frac{1}{2}$ kg	**ghee**

Steps

1. Prepare a nearly 2 string syrup by boiling the sugar and water.

2. Sieve both the flours together.

3. Heat 975 grams of the ghee in a deep vessel. When it starts fuming, reduce the heat to minimum.

4. Simultaneously, heat 150 gms of the ghee in a karahi and add to it the flour mixture. Fry on a slow flame, stirring all the time.

5. When the ghee starts separating add the sugar syrup. Mix well.

6. Add a serving spoon of hot ghee from the vessel to the flour-syrup mixture.

   Stir well. Repeat this 4-5 times. Finally, add all the ghee.

7. The mixture will become frothy and will not stick to the spoon. Turn it quickly on to a greased 2-3" deep metal tray.

8. Do not tilt or disturb the tray till the Mysore Pak is set and hard (5-7 minutes).

9. Raise one side of the tray. Cut and remove a small piece of Mysore Pak from one corner of the lower side. The Extra ghee will start flowing towards that side. Remove it.

10. Cut the Pak into square pieces.

Makes about 50 pieces.

LAVANG LATIKA

Requirements

For Filling	200 gms	khoya
	200 gms	paneer
	200 gms	powdered sugar
	50 gms	chopped mixed dry fruits like cashew, almond, chironji, raisin
	1/3 teaspoon	cardamom powder.
For Covering	500 gms	refined flour
	75 gms	ghee
		water for kneading
	40-45	cloves
For Coating :	500 gms	sugar
	2 cups	water
	6-8 drops	rose essence
	For Frying 700 gms	ghee

For decoration : 2-3 silver sheets.

Steps

1. Mash and mix the filling ingredients. Cook on a medium flame till the mixture dries up. Remove from the fire. Let it cool.

2. To prepare the dough for the covering, rub the 75 gms ghee into the refined flour. Add water and knead in to a tight pliable dough.

3. Prepare a two string syrup by boiling the sugar and water. When cold, add the essence.

4. Prepare balls the size of a leman from the dough. Roll each into a thin round. Place a table spoon full of filling in the centre. Moisten the edges of the round with water. Fold all the four sides towards the centre. Pin up the centre with a clove. Prepare all the lavang latikas in this manner.

5. Heat ghee in a Karahi. Deep fry lavang latikas on a medium flame. When golden brown in colour, drains and remove.

6. Dip the latikas in sugar syrup for 5-10 minutes. Drain and remove.

7. Decorate each with bits of silver sheets.

Makes 40-45 Lavang Latikas.

MALAI GHEWAR

Requirements

125 gms	**ghee**
$1\frac{1}{2}$ cups	**ice cold water**
500 gms	**refined flour**
1 liter	**milk**
$1\frac{1}{2}$ Kg	**ghee for frying**
1 kg	**sugar**
400 ml	**water**

For decoration :   1 lit thick sweetened milk (rabri), 1 tablespoon cardamom powder, 2 tablespoons chopped pistas, 2 tablespoons chironji

Steps

1. Rub 125 gms ghee in ice cold water.

2. Add the flour gradually, rubbing all the time. When the mixture becomes thick, keep adding milk gradually and alternately with the flour. The final mixture will be thin.

3. Heat 1 kg of the ghee in a thick, narrow and deep container or karahi. Keep aside the remaining ghee.

4. Take a large spoonfull of the flour batter, and pour it in a thin stream into the hot ghee (the quantity will depend on the size of the container or karahi and the size of ghewar required).

6. The mixture will spread all over the surface in a fine network.

7. Pour two spoonfulls from the remaining ghee around the rim of the karahi. The ghewar will rise up. Fry it to a light pink colour. Remove from the ghee with the help of two iron sticks. Prepare all the ghewars this way.

8. Keep the ghewars on a metal seive.

9. Boil sugar and water together to make a $1\frac{1}{2}$ string syrup. Cool it.

10. Pour the cold syrup on the ghewars. The excess will be drained through the sieve.

11. Before serving, pour a little *rabri* on each ghewar. Sprinkle cardamom powder over and decorate with chopped dry fruits.

Makes about 12-14 large Ghewar when each Ghewar is made out of 150 ml batter

Note: To make *rabri*, see recipe on page 106.

RABRI MALPUA

Requirements

600 gms	**sugar**
$2\frac{1}{3}$ cups	**water**
1 kg	**cow's milk**
75 gms	**refined flour**
6-8 threads	**saffron dissolved in a tablespoon of hot milk.**
500 gms	**ghee for frying**
1/2 teaspoon	**cardamom powder**
1 tablespoon	**chopped pistas**

Steps

1   Prepare a one string syrup by boiling the sugar and water.

2   Boil the milk. Remove the cream. Let the milk simmer on a slow flame, till reduced to 300 mls. Strain it through a seive.

3   Mix together the thickened milk (rabri), refined flour, saffron, cardamom and pista. Keep aside for an hour.

4   Heat ghee in a frying pan. Spread one serving spoonfull mixture in a round, in hot ghee. Fry on both sides to a brown colour, on a medium flame. Fry two-three malpuas at a time. Drain and remove.

5   Soak the malpuas in sugar syrup. Serve after half-an-hour.

Makes about 15-20 Malpuas.

Note

1   The Malpua mixture should be of a pouring consistency. Extra-flour or milk can be added to attain the required consistency.

2   To serve hot malpuas, keep the container in hot water.

3.   To make ordinary malpuas replace thickened milk with water or milk.

MAWE KI KACHORI

Requirements

For Filling:

150 gms	khoya
100 gms	powdered sugar
50 gms	chopped dry fruits like cashew, almond, chironji
1/4 teaspoon	nutmeg/cardamom powder

For Saffron Syrup:

250 gms	sugar
1 cup	water
8-10 threads	saffron dissolved in 2 tablespoons hot water.

For Covering:

250 gms	refined flour
1 tablespoon	gramflour
30 gms	ghee
	water for kneading
500 gms	ghee for deep frying.

Steps

1. Prepare the filling by mixing all the filling ingredients.

2. Prepare a two string sugar syrup by boiling the sugar and water. Add saffron water.

3. Mix gramflour and refined flour. Rub the 30 gms ghee into it. Prepare a medium-tight, pliable dough by adding a little water. Kneed for five minutes.

4. Prepare 15 balls of the dough. Flatten each. Fill a tablespoon of filling in each. Collect the extra dough on top, fold on one side. Flatten again evenly with the thumb ($2\frac{1}{2}$ - 3" diametre).

5. Heat ghee in a karahi. Cool it till it is just warm. Keeping on a slow flame, fry 3-4 kachories at a time on a slow to medium flame. Fry to a golden brown colour on both sides. Drain and remove.

6. Before serving, break the kachori lightly. Spread a tablespoon of saffron syrup over and serve.

Makes 15 Kachoris

MOHAN THAL

Requirements

1 cup	**milk**
25 gms	**ghee**
500 gms	**gram flour**
300 gms	**ghee**
100 gms	**khoya**
10-15 flakes	**saffron soaked in 2 tablespoon hot milk.**
$\frac{1}{2}$ teaspoon	**cardamom powder.**
400 gms	**sugar**
$1\frac{1}{2}$ ml	**water**

For decoration : 25 gms chopped dry fruits like cashews almonds and pistas.

Steps

1. Warm 1/4 cup of the milk and the 25 gms ghee. Mix and rub this into the sifted gramflour. Keep for 5-10 minutes.

2. Rub the mixture together and pass through a thick-holed metal sieve.

3. Heat ghee in a karahi, add gram crumbs and fry to a golden colour, on a medium flame.

4. Add mashed khoya and remaining milk to the mixture. Cook for 2-3 minutes then remove from the fire.

5. Add saffron milk and cardamom powder. Let the mixture cool.

6. Prepare a two string syrup by boiling the sugar and water.

7. Add sugar syrup to the gram mixture. Mix well.

8. Spread the mixture in a greased metal tray. Press down evenly.

9. Decorate by spreading dry fruits all over. Cut into pieces when slightly cold.

Makes 40-45 pieces.

PALANGTODH

Requirements

1 litre	**pure buffalo's milk**
4-6 pinches	**tartaric powder**
125 gms	**sugar**

For decoration : 1/2 silver sheet, 4 Pistas, chopped, 2 cardamoms, powdered

Steps

1. Boil milk in a karahi. Add pinches of tartaric powder to the boiling milk, till it begins to curdle and becomes slightly granular and rough. Tiny grains will appear on the back of a spoon, when it is stirred.

2. Keep boiling till the milk is reduced to half. Stir occasionally.

3. Add the sugar to the milk. Reduce the flame. Mix with a spatula.

4. When the mixture becomes semi solid, pinkish and frothy and starts leaving the sides of the karahi, remove from the fire.

5. Turn the mixture on to a greased metal box, 2" thick.

6. Immediately dip the lower half of the box in iced water. Remove and let it cool. The upper half of palang todh will be light brown in colour. While the portion dipped in ice-water will be white.

7. Loosing the sides with a knife and turn the palangtodh upside down.

8 Decorate with chopped pistas, cardamoms and the silver sheet.

9. Cut and serve.

Makes 6 pieces.

Note:

When round in shape, Palangtodh is also called malai cake.

If you want to make slightly softer palangtodh, a pinch of sodium Hydrosulphite can be added to the final mixture before removing it from the fire.

PATISA

Requirements

500 gms	ghee
250 gms	fine gramflour
250 gms	refined flour
625 gms	sugar
3 cups	water
2 tablespoons	milk

For decoration: 30 gms char magaz seeds, 2-3 large cardamoms peeled and seeds separated Square pieces from a transparent polythene sheet for wrapping.

Steps

1. Heat ghee in a karahi. Sift refined flour and gramflour together. Add to the ghee.

2. Fry to a light brown colour, on a slow flame. Remove from the fire. Let it cool.

3. Boil the sugar and water. Add milk to remove scum (dirt from sugar), strain the syrup and boil again to a $2\frac{1}{2}$ string consistency.

4. Add syrup quickly to the flour mixture. Mix well and beat with a fork to get a thread like structure (lach-chedar).

5. Immediately spread the mixture on a greased surface. Roll lightly with a rolling pin in to $1\frac{1}{2}$" thickness. Decorate with cardamom and charmagaz. Cut into square pieces and wrap in polythene pieces.

Makes around 45 pieces.

PEDA

Requirements

| 500 gms | **khoya** |
| 300 gms | **powdered sugar** |

For decoration: 1 teaspoon cardamom powder, 2 tablespoons chopped pista, a cookie mould.

Steps

1. Grate khoya and mix with the sugar.

2. Place the mixture in a karahi and cook for 5-7 minutes, on a medium to slow flame.

3. Keep stirring all the time. The mixture will thicken slightly.

4. Remove the karahi from the fire, mix in half the cardamom and let the mixture cool.

5. Divide the mixture into 35-40 balls.

6. Grease the mould. Sprinkle a pinch of cardamom and pista over. Press a ball of mixture, over it. Turn the mould down and carefully take out the Peda.

7. Prepare all the pedas this way.

Makes 35-40 Pedas.

Variations

USE DIFFERENT COLOURS AND FLAVOURS

Add any colour like yellow, red, orange or chocolate, to the peda mixture before putting into the moulds.

Add a few drops of any flavour like nutmeg, saffron, pineapple, orange, vanilla or almond. Decorate the top of the pedas with bits of almond, Pista, Chocolate, Cashew, Saffon thread, tutti-frutti or glazed cherry.

Contd. . . . . .

USE DRY FRUITS:

Add chopped dry fruits like almonds, cashews, walnuts, tutifrutti, or cherries to the peda mixture, before moulding.

USE DIFFERENT SWEETENING AGENTS

Use honey, brown sugar, caramel sugar or even molasses in place of sugar. This will provide a variety in taste and flavour.

USE DIFFERENT SHAPES

For moulding and shaping pedas, use cookie moulds of different shapes triangle, oblong or any other embossed surface.

PETHA

Requirements

$2\frac{1}{2}$ kg	**mature white pumpkin**
25 gms	**edible lime (calcium hydroxide)**
10 gms	**alum**
2 kgs	**sugar**
5 cups	**water**
1 tablespoon	**rose water**

Steps

1. Cut and peel the pumpkin. Remove seeds and mushy pulp. Cut the rest into strips and then in to 2 - $2\frac{1}{2}$" long pieces.

2. Poke the pieces all over with a metal skewer.

3. Dissolve lime in three litres of water. Strain it through a cloth, thrice.

4. Soak the pumpkin pieces in lime water for half an hour.

5. Remove the pumpkin from the lime water. Wash it thoroughly in running water 5-6 times.

6. Dissolve the alum in a cup of water and sprinkle over the pumpkin pieces.

7. Place the pieces in a large karahi and cook on a high flame. The pieces will exude water. When the mixture starts boiling and is slightly cooked, and soft, remove from the heat. Drain and wash the pieces again in running water.

8. Boil the sugar in 5 cups water. Add 3-4 tablespoons of milk to cut the scum. Strain the syrup through a fine strainer. Boil again to a thick ball consistency.

9. Add the pumkin pieces to the syrup. Boil on a medium flame till the syrup thickens again. Take off the fire and keep overnight.

10. The next day, remove the pieces from the syrup. Boil the syrup again to a thick consistency. Put the pieces back in the syrup. Let it boil for a minute or two. Remove from the fire.

11. When the petha is cold, sprinkle over the rose water.

Makes about 3 Kg. Petha.

Contd.....

Variations:

ANGOORI PETHA

To make this, the pumpkin pieces are cut in $2\frac{1}{2}$" long cylinders. While the syrup is boiling it should be thin (of a two string consistency). This makes the petha soft and full of syrup.

KESARI ANGOORI PETHA

15 to 20 strings of saffron are dissolved in 1/4 cup of hot milk, which is added to the syrup while cooking the petha on the second day.

RABRI (BASUNDI)

Requirements

2 litres	**full cream buffalo's milk**
175 grams	**sugar**
8-10 strings	**saffron**

For decoration : 1/4 tea spoon cardamom powder, 20 grams almonds, 10 grams pista, 1 silver sheet

Steps

1. Boil milk in a large heavy bottomed karahi. Keep stirring frequently. When reduced by half add the sugar and the saffron keep boiling and stirring on a slow flame.

2. When reduced to 800 ml (even up to 600 ml for very thick rabri) remove from the fire.

3. Decorate with chopped dry fruits, cardamom and silver sheet. Refrigerate and serve cold.

SANDESH

Requirements

1 litre	**milk**
1	**lemon**
1 teaspoon	**refined flour**
3-4 tablespoons	**powdered sugar**
1/8 teaspoon	**rose essence**
1 teaspoon	**chopped pistas**
1/4 teaspoon	**cardamom powder**
	few cookie moulds, lightly greased

Steps:

1. Boil the milk and keep for 6 hours. Remove the cream from it .

2. Boil the milk again. Add lemon juice to it till it curdles.

3. Turn in to a muslin cloth and dip it in cold water for 10 minutes. Remove and hang it up to remove water for about an hour.

4. Take out the cheese. Rub well for about 10 minutes till soft and smooth. Add refined flour and mix well.

5. Mix the cheese and sugar in a karahi. Cook on a medium to slow flame. Keep stirring.

6. In 6-8 minutes the mixture will become semi-thick. Remove from the fire. Mix in essence.

7. Grease the moulds. Sprinkle a pinch of cardamom and some pista at the base. Fill sandesh mixture in it. Gently turn onto a plate. Prepare all the sandesh this way.

8. Makes about 8-9 Sandesh Store in the refrigerator and serve cold.

Variations:

1. Use different colours like green, red, orange, yellow, chocolate to make differently coloured Sandesh. Use decorative moulds for variety in shape.

2. Use different flavours like vanilla, saffron, kewra, pineapple, lemon, orange, mango to get variety in flavour. Correspondingly, use bits like lemon, orange, mango and pineapple for decoration.

3. Use chopped dry fruits like cashews, almonds, chironji dates, fresh grated coconut in the sandesh mixture. Decorate accordingly. Use of cocoa and chocolate chips gives a unique flavour to the sandesh.

4. Use honey instead of sugar to give a wonderful taste and flovour to sandesh.

SHRIKHAND

Requirements

1 kilogram	**fresh, thick curds made from buffalo's milk**
200-250 gms	**sugar (depending on**
	sourness of the curds)
1/2 teaspoon	**cardamom powder**
20 grams	**chironji**

Steps

1. Hang curd in a clean muslin cloth for 6-8 hours, to remove all the water. This thick curd is called 'chakka'. It is a requirement for any shrikhand.

2. Mix together the chakka and sugar. Use a mixer or pass the mixture through a steel sieve.

3. Add chironji and cardamom. Refrigerate for 2-3 hours before serving makes 400-450 gram of shrikand.

Variations:

KESARI OR SAFFRON SHRIKHAND

Dissolve 6-8 strings of saffron in a tablespoon of hot milk. Add this to the shrikhand.

NUTMEG OR JAIPHAL SHRIKHAND

Dissolve 1/4 teaspoon of nutmeg powder in a tablespoon of hot milk. Add this to the shrikhand.

FRUIT SHRIKHAND

Mix 100 grams of any of the following fruit cleaned, peeled and chopped: eg. mango, orange, banana, pineapple, grapes. Instead of mango pieces, ripe mango pulp can also be added. If fruit is not available, essences can be used.

DRY FRUIT SHRIKHAND

Mix in 100 grams of chopped dry fruit, mixed or any one like cashews, almonds, raisins, pistas.